D1377428

EARTH'S CYCLES

The Food Cycle

CHERYL JAKAB

A+

Smart Apple Media

This edition first published in 2008 in the United States of America by Smart Apple Media.
All rights reserved. No part of this book may be reproduced in any form or by any means without written permission from the publisher.

Smart Apple Media
2140 Howard Drive West
North Mankato, Minnesota 56003

First published in 2007 by
MACMILLAN EDUCATION AUSTRALIA PTY LTD
627 Chapel Street, South Yarra, Australia 3141

Visit our Web site at www.macmillan.com.au or go directly to www.macmillanlibrary.com.au

Associated companies and representatives throughout the world.

Copyright © Cheryl Jakab 2007

Library of Congress Cataloging-in-Publication Data

Jakab, Cheryl.
    The food cycle / by Cheryl Jakab.
    p. cm. — (Earth's cycles)
    Includes index.
    ISBN 978-1-59920-149-8
    1. Food chains (Ecology)—Juvenile literature. I. Title.

QH541.15.F66.J35 2007
577'.16—dc22

2007004554

Edited by Erin Richards
Text and cover design by Christine Deering
Page layout by Christine Deering
Photo research by Jes Senbergs
Illustrations by Ann Likhovetsky, pp. 10, 13, 18, 19; Paul Könye, p. 29.

Printed in U.S.

Acknowledgements
The author and the publisher are grateful to the following for permission to reproduce copyright material:

Front cover photographs: giant panda eating bamboo (center), courtesy of Jean-Paul Ferrero/Auscape; worms (background), courtesy of Photodisc.

Keith Weller/Agricultural Research Service, p. 11 (main); Dennis Cox/Alamy, p. 26; Juniors Bildarchiv/Alamy, p. 23 (bottom); Theo Allofs/Auscape, p. 19; Tui De Roy/Auscape, p. 7; Jean-Paul Ferrero/Auscape, pp. 1, 5, 17 (bottom); Jean-Michel Labat/Auscape, p. 28 (top); Corbis, pp. 4 (middle right & top left), 20 (middle left & middle right); Momatiuk-Eastcott/Corbis, p. 9; Rob Cruse, p. 23 (top); CDC/James Gathany, p. 6 (top); altrendo nature/Getty Images, p. 21 (top); Rob Gage/Getty Images, p. 27; Klaus Nigge/Getty Images, p. 28 (bottom); Joseph van Os/Getty Images, p. 14 (top); Anup Shah/Getty Images, pp. 6 (left), 12; iStockphoto.com, p. 22 (bottom); Peter & Margy Nicholas/Lochman Transparencies, p. 22 (top); Len Stewart/Lochman Transparencies, p. 21 (bottom); Dave Watts/Lochman Transparencies, p. 14 (bottom); NASA, pp. 4 (center), 30; Niall Benvie/Nature Picture Library, p. 16; NOAA, p. 25; Bob Bennett/OSF images, p. 15 (both); Photodisc, pp. 4 (bottom left, bottom right, middle left & top right), 8, 11 (insert), 13, 20 (bottom left, bottom right, center & top), 24; Photolibrary, p. 6 (right), Photos.com, p. 17 (top).

While every care has been taken to trace and acknowledge copyright, the publisher tenders their apologies for any accidental infringement where copyright has proved untraceable. Where the attempt has been unsuccessful, the publisher welcomes information that would redress the situation.

Contents

Glossary words
When a word is printed in **bold**, you can look up its meaning in the glossary on page 31.

Earth's natural cycles

What is a cycle?

A cycle is a never-ending series of changes that repeats again and again. Arrows in cycle diagrams show the direction in which the cycle is moving.

Earth's natural cycles create every environment on Earth. Living and non-living things are constantly changing. Each change is part of a natural cycle. Earth's natural cycles are working all the time.

Earth's non-living cycles are:
- the water cycle
- the rock cycle
- the seasons cycle

Earth's living cycles are:
- the food cycle
- the animal life cycle
- the plant life cycle

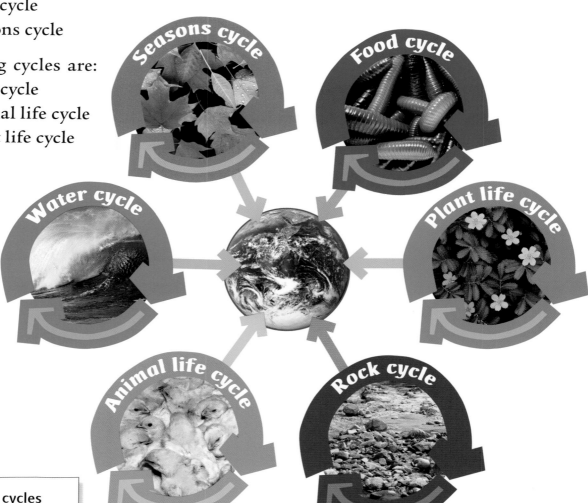

Seasons cycle

Food cycle

Water cycle

Plant life cycle

Animal life cycle

Rock cycle

Earth's natural cycles keep the planet healthy.

The balance of nature

Earth's natural cycles all connect with each other. The way the cycles connect is sometimes called the balance of nature.

Keeping the balance

Every living thing depends on Earth's natural cycles to survive. A change in one cycle can affect the whole balance of nature. Knowing how Earth's cycles work helps us keep the environment healthy.

Every living thing depends on the balance of nature to survive.

Food

What is food?

Food is any substance used by a living thing to give it energy.
Every living thing can be a source of food for another living thing.

Living things need food to survive. Food gives living things the **nutrients** they need to live and grow. Sandwiches in your lunchbox are food. Leaves eaten by a giraffe and fish caught by a bear are food. Even blood taken by a mosquito from another animal is food for the mosquito.

Mosquitoes get energy from the blood they take from other animals.

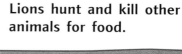

Giraffes have very long necks to reach the leaves they eat.

Lions hunt and kill other animals for food.

6

The importance of food

Food is a very important part of the natural environment.
Every living thing on Earth needs food to grow and live.

Why is food important to people?

People are living things that need food to survive. People eat food from plants, such as vegetables and nuts. They also eat meat, such as steak from a cow. Fungi, such as mushrooms, are another source of food.

How do people affect the food cycle?

People clear land to build towns and for farms. This loss of **habitat** makes it harder for plants and animals to find food.

How does food fit into the balance of nature?

Each natural habitat on Earth has its own particular food chain. One broken link in a food chain can affect all the plants and animals in that habitat.

Wetlands provide food for many different animals, such as flamingos.

7

The food cycle

The food cycle shows the different stages that food moves through in the natural environment. Plants make food, using energy from the sun and nutrients from the soil. Plants are food for plant-eating animals. Meat eaters eat other animals for food. **Decomposers** complete the cycle by feeding on the remains of dead plants and animals. They turn the remains into soil for plants to grow.

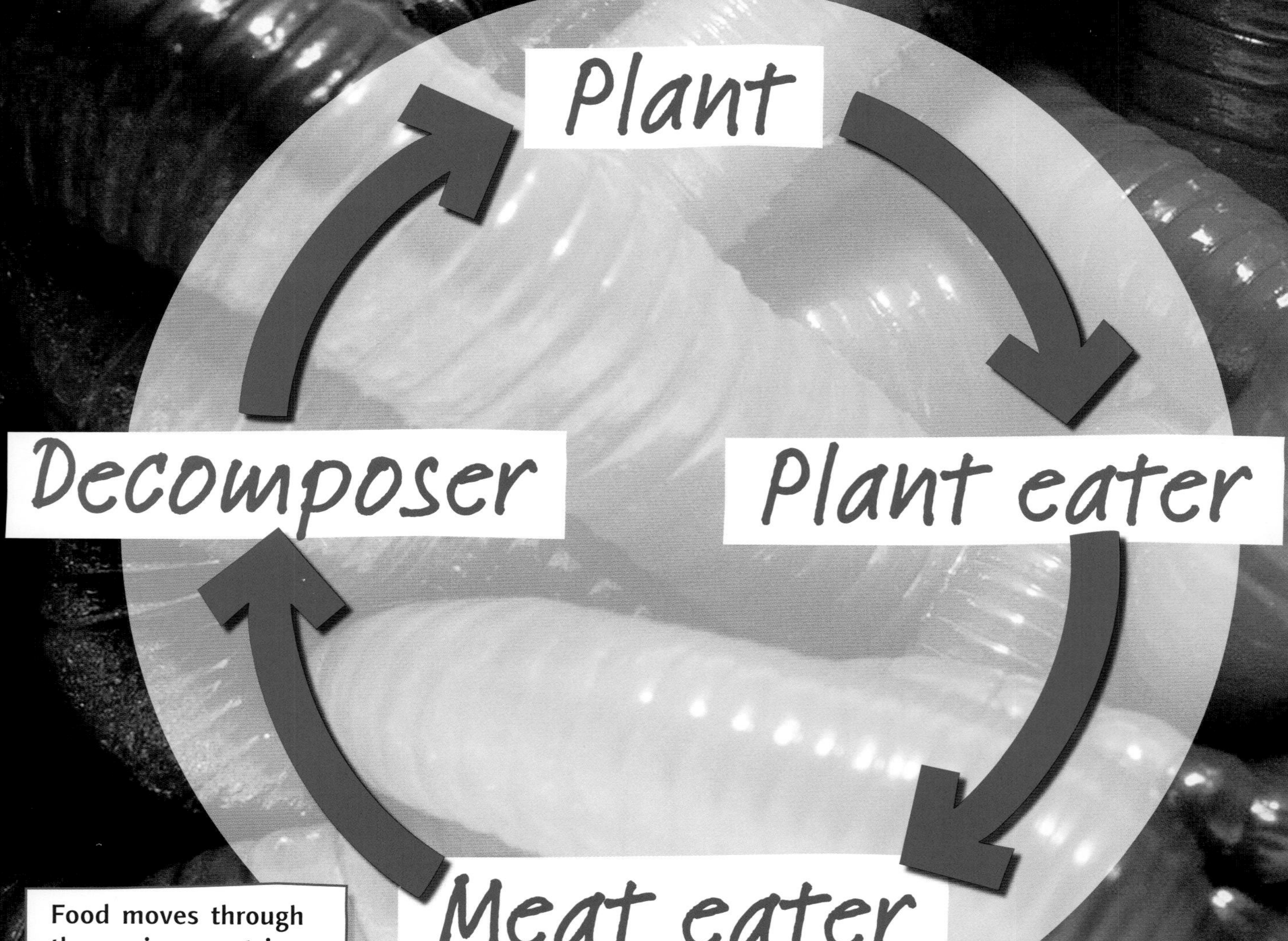

Plant

Plant eater

Meat eater

Decomposer

Food moves through the environment in a never-ending cycle.

8

Energy from the sun

The original source of most food energy on Earth is sunlight from the sun. Sunlight gives plants the energy they need to make food. Energy from the sun is called solar energy.

The sun is the source of energy for most plants to make food.

Plant

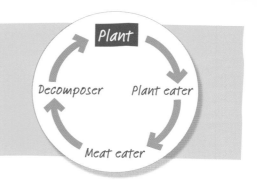

In the first stage of the food cycle, plants make their own food. Plants are the producers in the food cycle because they produce food for themselves.

A plant produces its own food through a process called photosynthesis. The roots of the plant take up water and nutrients from the soil. The leaves take in **carbon dioxide** from the air. The water and carbon dioxide combine to make sugars, which are food for the plant. Sunlight from the sun provides the energy for photosynthesis.

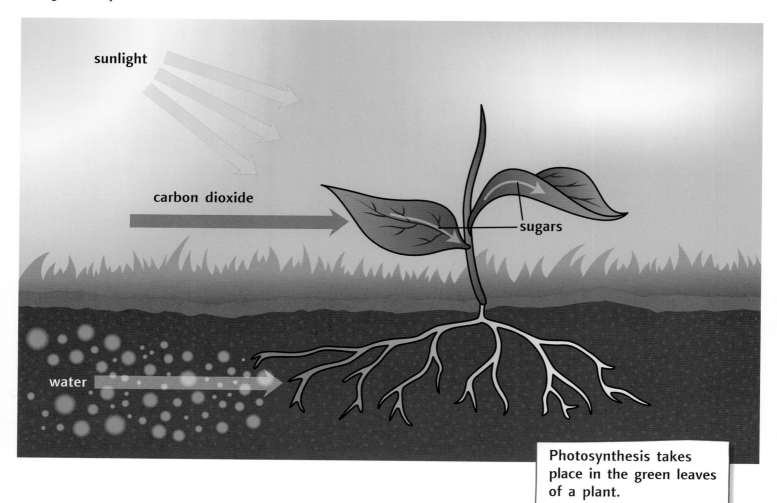

Photosynthesis takes place in the green leaves of a plant.

Storing food

Plants use the food they make to live and grow. Extra food is stored in their roots, stems, leaves, fruits, and seeds. Plants use these food stores when there is less sunlight for photosynthesis to take place, such as in winter.

Plants need to be in sunlight to produce food.

Many plants store food in their fruits, such as these cherries.

Plant eater

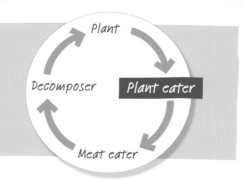

Plant-eating animals eat plants in the next stage of the food cycle. Animals that eat only plants are called herbivores. They eat all the different parts of plants, including the leaves, stems, roots, fruits, and seeds.

Herbivores can be tiny, such as millipedes, caterpillars, and some snails and insects. They can also be very big animals, such as elephants, buffalo, and gorillas. Many herbivores eat particular types of plants. Giant pandas eat only bamboo shoots. Koalas eat only eucalyptus leaves.

Gorillas are herbivores because they eat only plants.

Sheep spend most of each day grazing.

Digestion

Animals are the consumers of the food cycle. They get their food by eating, or consuming, other living things. Animals get nutrients from their food through a process called digestion. Some foods, such as the leaves and stems of many plants, are not very rich in nutrients. Animals that eat them must digest a lot of food to get enough energy to live and grow. This is why many herbivores spend a lot of their time eating.

Animals digest their food to give them energy to live and grow.

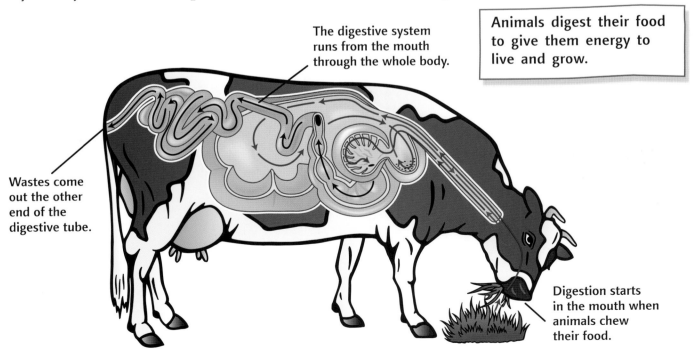

The digestive system runs from the mouth through the whole body.

Wastes come out the other end of the digestive tube.

Digestion starts in the mouth when animals chew their food.

Meat eater

In the next stage of the food cycle, plant eaters are food for meat eaters. Meat-eating animals are called carnivores. Carnivores can be big, such as lions, sharks, and crocodiles, or small, such as praying mantises. Some carnivores hunt and kill their food and others **scavenge** for it.

Carnivores that hunt and kill are called **predators**. Predators have bodies that are good for hunting. Many have sharp teeth and large claws. Some predators run very fast to catch their **prey**.

A lion has sharp teeth and claws to help it catch and kill its prey.

Sea eagles are carnivores that hunt and kill other animals.

14

Omnivores

Omnivores are animals that consume both plants and animals. People are omnivores, since the human body is able to digest both plant and animal foods. Some people do not like to eat animals. They prefer to eat only plant foods. These people are called vegetarians. Some vegetarians eat eggs and other animal products, but not meat. Vegetarians who do not eat any animal products are called vegans.

Some animals, such as grizzly bears, eat both plants and animals.

Bears catch fish to eat as well as eating plants.

15

Decomposer

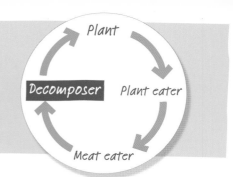

In this stage of the food cycle, decomposers feed on dead plants and animals. As decomposers feed, plant and animal bodies rot, or decompose. The nutrients inside the plants and animals are recycled back into the soil. Without decomposers, the nutrients in dead plants and animals would be trapped inside them. The dead material would not be recycled, and the food cycle would not be complete.

Decomposers recycle leaf remains back into the soil.

Fungi, bacteria, and soil animals

Decomposers include **bacteria**, molds, soil animals, and fungi, such as mushrooms. Mushrooms seen above the ground are only small parts of the fungi. Most of a mushroom is underground, feeding on rotting plant and animal material.

Fungi feed on rotting plant and animal material.

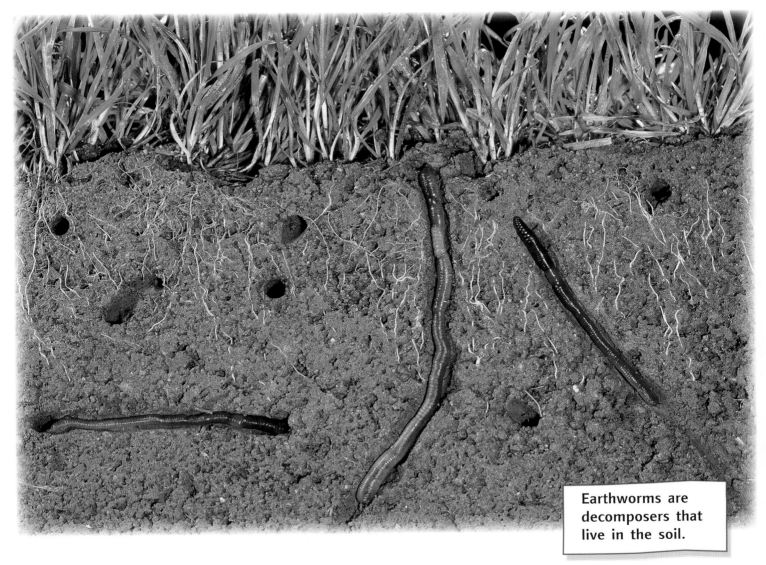

Earthworms are decomposers that live in the soil.

Food chains, webs, and pyramids

Food in a habitat

Food chains, food webs, and food pyramids are ways of showing how living things in a natural habitat are linked by feeding.

Food chains

Food chains show how two or more living things are linked by feeding. Seaweed is food for a small fish. The small fish is food for a bigger fish. This is a simple food chain.

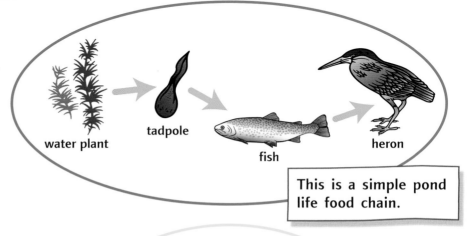

This is a simple pond life food chain.

Food webs

Food webs are used to show all the food chains in a particular habitat. Food webs often look very messy, with links crossing over each other. A complete food web shows all the plants, plant eaters, meat eaters, and decomposers that live in a habitat. Complete food webs can be quite complex.

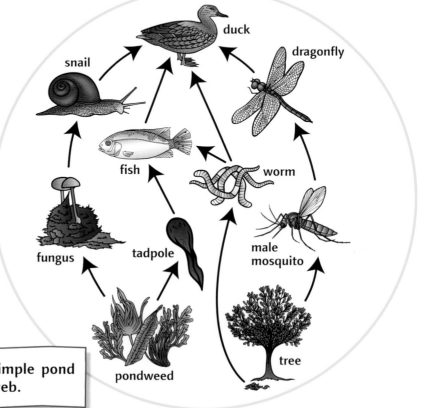

This is a simple pond life food web.

Food pyramids

Food pyramids are narrow at the top and wide at the bottom. Meat eaters are at the top of a food pyramid, because they exist in the smallest numbers. Plant eaters are shown on the next level down, and plants are below the plant eaters. If decomposers are shown, they are put at the bottom of a pyramid. There are more decomposers in a habitat than producers and consumers.

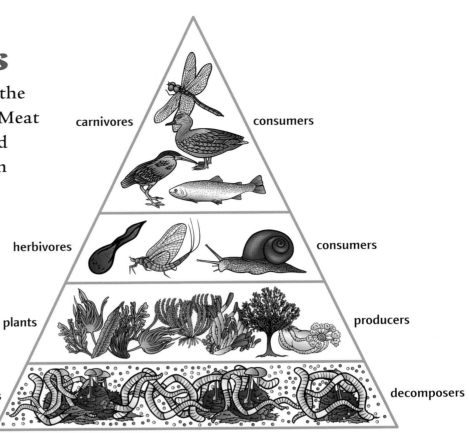

carnivores — consumers

herbivores — consumers

plants — producers

decomposers — decomposers

This is a simple pond life food pyramid.

A wading bird finds food in a pond habitat.

The balance of nature

The balance of nature shows how the food cycle is linked with Earth's other cycles. The food cycle has an effect on non-living and living things in every environment on Earth. The seasons, animals, plants, rocks, and water all help maintain the food cycle.

The food cycle is an important part of the balance of nature.

Food and the seasons

The amount of food that is available changes with the seasons. In most habitats, plants produce less food during winter. Plants usually grow more in spring and summer, and many fruits ripen in fall. As the seasons change, some animals **migrate** to areas where food is available.

The fruits of many plants ripen in fall.

Food, rocks, and soil

The mineral nutrients in food come from rocks and soil. Plants grow in the soil, and take up nutrients and water through their roots. Soil is a mixture of tiny bits of rock, plant and animal material, decomposers, air, and water. Rich **fertile** soil contains many nutrients and can grow more plants.

Carrots get the nutrients they need to grow from the soil.

Food and water

All plants need water to survive. In places with a lot of water, such as rivers, lakes, oceans, and wetlands, there are often rich habitats. These areas have many plants that provide rich feeding grounds for many animals. In deserts, where there is little water, less plant material can grow, and there is less food for animals. Desert plants and animals are adapted to living with little water.

Many animals live near coral reefs where there is plenty of food.

Camels store food in their humps to use when desert plants are hard to find.

Food and plants

Plants provide food for many animals, including humans.
People eat food from all the different parts of plants, including:

- seeds of plants, such as beans, wheat, rice, and corn
- roots of plants, such as onions, carrots, and potatoes
- stems of plants, such as celery and sugar cane
- leaves of plants, such as lettuce and spinach
- fruits of plants, such as pineapples, apples, oranges, and tomatoes

fruits

roots

Plants store food in all their different parts.

stems

seeds

Food and animals

Animals produce young when there is a good food supply. When there are more plants, the plant eaters will reproduce. More plant-eating animals means more food for meat eaters, and they also reproduce. A natural balance develops between food supply and animal numbers.

With a good food supply in the habitat, wild boar piglets are more likely to survive.

People and food

People need food to survive. The bigger the world population gets the more food is needed, now and in the future. However, some human activities are damaging the food cycle. Polluting land and water and overfishing can break links in food chains and affect a whole habitat.

Pollution

Ocean habitats are polluted by oil spills and waste water flowing into the sea. Tiny amounts of **pollutants** are absorbed by ocean plants and build up in the animals that eat them. As the food chain progresses, meat eaters can end up with dangerous levels of pollutants in their bodies. High levels of pollutants in an animal can make them poisonous to anyone who eats them.

Pollutants can build up in sharks because they are at the top of the food chain.

Overfishing

Fish numbers are declining in the oceans due to overfishing. Modern fishing fleets have large ships that clean and freeze up to 110 tons (100 t) of fish at a time. These ships work fishing grounds for many months at a time. Overfishing is causing many fish **species** to become **endangered**. In the year 2000, cod was added to the endangered species list because of overfishing. Today, halibut, herring, cod, salmon, anchovies, and sardines are all being overfished.

Overfishing is reducing fish numbers in the oceans.

Protecting food cycles

Today, many people are working to protect natural food cycles. Farming fish and protecting natural habitats are two ways of maintaining food cycles. **Sustainable** farming is also important to the future of the food cycle.

Farming fish

Farming fish instead of catching them from the oceans can help provide food for people without overfishing. Fish eggs can be hatched and the young fish put into pens where they are fed. Atlantic salmon in Norway and marine shrimps in Ecuador are farmed in this way. This reduces the need to catch them from the oceans.

Protecting natural habitats

Natural habitats often contain many different plant and animal species. Protecting natural habitats allows food cycles to continue, and maintains the balance of nature. Today, whole areas are being set aside as national parks and wildlife reserves to protect natural food cycles.

Wildlife reserves help keep some habitat for giant pandas to live in.

Rice paddies are cut into hillsides to get higher yields of rice from one piece of land.

Sustainable farming

As the human population on Earth increases, more food needs to be grown without damaging the environment. Sustainable farming keeps soil fertile while giving high **yields**. Today, about one-third of the land on Earth is used to grow food for people. Sustainable farming methods allow an increase in food production without using up more land and damaging the environment.

Protecting local food cycles

Everyone can help protect food cycles. Getting active can help protect natural food cycles in your area.

Gardening is a great way to learn about plants and the animals that eat them.

Get active

- Learn about food webs in your area
- Visit a local national park or wildlife reserve
- Buy foods grown **organically**
- Add plants to your garden for local wildlife to eat
- Do not use poisons, such as weed killers, on your garden
- Find out if the foods you eat are produced using sustainable farming methods

A grub from your garden could become food for hungry chicks.

Make a bird feeder

Safety note: Ask an adult before using scissors.

Make a bird feeder for your garden. Only supply a small amount of food though, so birds do not come to depend on the food source.

What you need

- an empty milk carton
- some wire
- a dowel
- bird food
- scissors

What to do

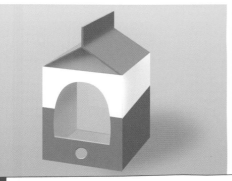

1 Cut openings in the milk carton at the front and at the back. Make a small hole underneath each opening for the dowel.

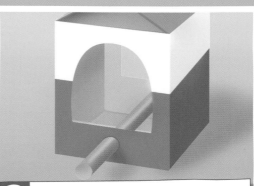

2 Push the dowel through the small holes. Leave enough poking out for birds to use as a perch.

3 Place a small amount of bird food in the bottom of the carton. You can buy bird food from a store or try making your own mix.

4 Use wire to hang the bird feeder in the garden. Hang it up high so predators, such as cats, cannot get to it easily.

Which foods make the best bird food mix?

Living with nature

We all depend on the balance of nature for our survival. If people continue to disturb Earth's cycles, it will upset the balance of nature. Understanding Earth's cycles helps us care for Earth and live in harmony with nature.

"The Earth does not belong to us: we belong to the Earth."

(Chief Seattle Suquamish leader, about 1854)

Glossary

bacteria	microscopic decomposers
carbon dioxide	gas that plants take from the air as they live and grow
decomposers	living things that break down dead plant and animal material
endangered	in danger of dying out
fertile	rich in the minerals and nutrients needed to grow plants
habitat	place where plants and animals naturally grow and live
migrate	move from one place to another
nutrients	substances that give living things energy to live and grow
organically	without using man-made chemicals
pollutants	materials that pollute the air, water, or soil
predators	animals that hunt, kill, and eat other animals
prey	animals that are killed and eaten by other animals
scavenge	feed on the remains of dead animals
species	a particular type of plant or animal
sustainable	able to be continued without damaging the environment
yields	amounts of food produced

Index